Read for a
Better World™

THE SCHOOL LIBRARY

MARGO GATES

GRL Consultants,
Diane Craig and Monica Marx,
Certified Literacy Specialists

Lerner Publications ◆ Minneapolis

Educator Toolbox

Reading books is a great way for kids to express what they're interested in. Before reading this title, ask the reader these questions:

> What do you think this book is about? Look at the cover for clues.

> What do you already know about the school library?

> What do you want to find out about the school library?

Let's Read Together

Encourage the reader to use the pictures to understand the text.

Point out when the reader successfully sounds out a word.

Praise the reader for recognizing sight words such as *find* and *we*.

TABLE OF CONTENTS

The School Library 4

The School Library

Today we visit the school library. Our teacher takes us there.

We meet the librarian.

She helps us find many kinds of books.

Some books teach us facts. Some books tell stories that are made up.

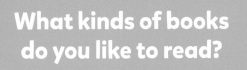

What kinds of books do you like to read?

9

Here is where we listen to audiobooks.

Here are the computers.

We use them to find facts.

Some parts of the
library are quiet.
We try not to talk.

Why do you think
it is important to be
quiet in a library?

Some libraries have places to build and create.

We pick out books
to take home.

The librarian helps us.

We take care of our books.
We will return them to the library soon!

You Connect!

What is your favorite part of your school library?

How do you find the books you want at your school library?

What would you like to build or create in a library?

Social and Emotional Snapshot

Student voice is crucial to building reader confidence. Ask the reader:

> What is your favorite part of this book?

> What is something you learned from this book?

> Did this book remind you of your own school library?

Opportunities for social and emotional learning are everywhere. How can you connect the topic of this book to the SEL competencies below?

Self-Awareness
Relationship Skills
Social Awareness

Photo Glossary

audiobook

book

computer

librarian

Learn More

Funk, Josh. *Lost in the Library: A Story of Patience & Fortitude*. New York: Henry Holt and Company, 2018.

Gates, Margo. *The School Bus*. Minneapolis: Lerner Publications, 2023.

Rustad, Martha E. H. *Sam Visits the School Library*. Minneapolis: Millbrook Press, 2018.

Index

Photo Acknowledgments

The images in this book are used with the permission of: © phi2/iStockphoto, pp. 14–15; © Ridofranz/iStockphoto, pp. 13, 20; © SDI Productions/iStockphoto, pp. 6, 10–11, 16–17, 23 (audio book, librarian); © Sergey Novikov/Shutterstock Images, p. 7; © Tyler Olson/Shutterstock Images, p. 19; © wavebreakmedia/Shutterstock Images, pp. 4–5, 8–9, 12, 18, 23 (book), 23 (computer).

Cover Photo: FatCamera/iStockphoto.

Design Elements: © Mighty Media, Inc.

Lerner Publications Company
An imprint of Lerner Publishing Group, Inc.
241 First Avenue North
Minneapolis, MN 55401 USA

For reading levels and more information, look up this title at www.lernerbooks.com.

Main body text set in Mikado a Medium.
Typeface provided by Hannes von Doehren.

Library of Congress Cataloging-in-Publication Data

Names: Gates, Margo, author.
Title: The school library / Margo Gates.
Description: Minneapolis : Lerner Publications, [2023] | Series: Read about school (Read for a better world) | Includes bibliographical references and index. | Audience: Ages 5–8. | Audience: Grades K–1. | Summary: "School libraries are the hub for learning, community, and creating. Full-color photos and kid-friendly text highlight all the things a library can be"– Provided by publisher.
Identifiers: LCCN 2021043447 (print) | LCCN 2021043448 (ebook) | ISBN 9781728459295 (library binding) | ISBN 9781728464244 (paperback) | ISBN 9781728461854 (ebook)
Subjects: LCSH: Libraries—Juvenile literature. | School libraries—Juvenile literature.
Classification: LCC Z665.5 .G38 2023 (print) | LCC Z665.5 (ebook) | DDC 027.8—dc23/eng/20211109

LC record available at https://lccn.loc.gov/2021043447
LC ebook record available at https://lccn.loc.gov/2021043448

Manufactured in the United States of America
1 - CG - 7/15/22